Shoes

Memories of a Lifetime™

ARTWORK FOR SCRAPBOOKS AND FABRIC-TRANSFER CRAFTS

Karey Judd

A LARK/CHAPELLE BOOK
A Division of Sterling Publishing Co., Inc.
New York

A Lark/Chapelle Book

Author: Karey Judd

Chapelle, Ltd., Inc.
P.O. Box 9255, Ogden, UT 84409
(801) 621-2777 • (801) 621-2788 Fax
e-mail: chapelle@chapelleltd.com
Web site: www.chapelleltd.com

10 9 8 7 6 5 4 3 2 1

First Edition

Published by Lark Books, A Division of
Sterling Publishing Co., Inc.
387 Park Avenue South, New York, N.Y. 10016

Distributed in Canada by Sterling Publishing, c/o Canadian Manda Group,
165 Dufferin Street, Toronto, Ontario, Canada M6K 3H6

Distributed in the United Kingdom by GMC Distribution Services,
Castle Place, 166 High Street, Lewes, East Sussex, England BN7 1XU

Distributed in Australia by Capricorn Link (Australia) Pty Ltd.,
P.O. Box 704, Windsor, NSW 2756 Australia

PC Configuration: Windows 98 or later with 128 MB RAM or greater. At least 100 MB of free hard-disk space. Dual speed or faster CD-ROM drive, and a 24-bit color monitor.

Macintosh Configuration: Mac OS 9 or later with 128 MB RAM or greater. At least 100 MB of free hard-disk space. Dual speed or faster CD-ROM drive, and a 24-bit color monitor.

Manufactured in China

ISBN 13: 978-1-57990-982-6
ISBN 10: 1-57990-982-5

For information about custom editions, special sales, premium and corporate purchases, please contact Sterling Special Sales Department at 800-805-5489 or specialsales@sterlingpub.com.

InTroducTion

Imagine having hundreds of rare vintage images right at your fingertips. With our *Memories of a Lifetime*™ series, that's exactly what you get. We've scoured antique stores, estate sales, and other outlets to find one-of-a-kind images to give your projects the flair that only old-time artwork can provide. From Victorian postcards to hand-painted beautiful borders and frames, it would take years to acquire a collection like this. However, with this easy-to-use resource, you'll have them all—right here, right now.

Each image has been reproduced to the highest quality standard for photocopying and scanning; reduce or enlarge them to suit your needs. A CD-ROM containing all of the images in digital form is included, enabling you to use them for any computer project over and again. If you prefer to use them as they're printed, simply cut them out—they're printed on one side only.

Perfect for paper crafting, scrapbooking, and fabric transfers, *Memories of a Lifetime* books will inspire you to explore new avenues of creativity. We've included a sampling of ideas to get you started, but the best part is using your imagination to create your own fabulous projects. Be sure to look for other books in this series as we continue to search the markets for wonderful vintage images.

How to Use This Book

General Instructions:

These images are printed on one side only, making it easy to simply cut out the desired image. However, you'll probably want to use them again, so we have included a CD-ROM which contains all of the images individually as well as in the page layout form. The CDs can be used with both PC and Mac formats. Just pop in the disk. On a PC, the file will immediately open to the Home page, which will walk you through how to view and print the images.

For Macintosh® users, you will simply double-click on the icon to open. The images may also be incorporated into your computer projects using simple imaging software that you can purchase specifically for this purpose—a perfect choice for digital scrapbooking.

The reference numbers printed on the back of each image in the book are the same ones used on the CD, which will allow you to easily find the image you are looking for. The numbering consists of the book abbreviation, the page number, the image number, and the file format. The first file number (located next to the page number) is for the entire page. For example, SH01-001.jpg would be the entire image for page 1 of *Shoes*. These are provided for you on the CD. The second file number is for the top-right image. The numbers continue in a counterclock-wise spiral fashion.

Once you have resized your images, added text, created a scrapbook page, etc., you are ready to print them out. Printing on cream or white cardstock, particularly a textured variety, creates a more authentic look. You won't be able to tell that it's a reproduction! If you don't have access to a computer or printer, that's ok. Most photocopy centers can resize and print your images for a nominal fee, or they have do-it-yourself machines that are easy to use.

Ideas for Using the Images:

Scrapbooking: These images are perfect for both heritage and modern scrapbook pages. Simply use the image as a frame, accent piece, or border. For those of you with limited time, the page layouts in this book have been created so that you can use them as they are. Simply print out or photocopy the desired page, attach a photograph into one of the boxes, and you have a beautiful scrapbook page in minutes. For a little dimension, add a ribbon or charm. Be sure to print your images onto acid-free cardstock so the pages will last a lifetime.

Cards: Some computer programs allow images to be inserted into a card template, simplifying cardmaking. If this is not an option, simply use the images as accent pieces on the front or inside of the card. Use a bone folder to score the card's fold to create a more professional look.

Decoupage/Collage Projects: For decoupage or collage projects, photocopy or print the image onto a thinner paper such as copier paper. Thin paper adheres to projects more effectively. Decoupage medium glues and seals the project, creating a gloss or matte finish when dry, thus protecting the image. Vintage images are beautiful when decoupaged to cigar boxes, glass plates, and even wooden plaques. The possibilities are endless.

Fabric Arts: Vintage images can be used in just about any fabric craft imaginable: wall hangings, quilts, bags, or baby bibs. Either transfer the image onto the fabric by using a special iron-on paper, or by printing the image directly onto the fabric, using a temporary iron-on stabilizer that stabilizes the fabric to feed through a printer. These items are available at most craft and sewing stores. If the item will be washed, it is better to print directly on the fabric. For either method, follow the instructions on the package.

Wood Transfers: It is now possible to "print" images on wood. Use this exciting technique to create vintage plaques, clocks, frames, and more. A simple, inexpensive transfer tool is available at most large craft or home improvement stores, or online from various manufacturers. You simply place the photocopy of the image you want, face down, onto the surface and use the tool to transfer the image onto the wood. This process requires a copy from a laser printer, which means you will probably have to get your copies made at a copy center. Refer to manufacturer's instructions for additional details. There are other transfer products available that can be used with wood. Choose the one that is easiest for you.

Gallery of Ideas

These images can be used in a variety of projects: cards, scrapbook pages, and decoupage projects to name a few. The images can be used as they are shown in the layout, or you can copy and clip out individual images, or even portions or multitudes of images. The following pages contain a collection of ideas to inspire you to use your imagination and create one-of-a-kind treasures.

Keepsakes

With some creativity and embellishing, cigar boxes and small containers become treasure chests for special mementos.

Favorite Things

Make a personal journal for recording your thoughts or favorite things by adorning a simple notebook. Antique advertisements, ribbons, tags, and decorative paper create an attractive look.

Greeting Cards

Tags with antique images make eye-catching embellishments to gifts. Simply cut out the images and adhere them to decorative cardstock. Add ribbon for a delicate touch.

Framed Prints

The decorative pages in this book make attractive backgrounds for favorite photographs. For a graceful, timeworn look, add a bow and place the matted photograph in a weathered frame.

Paired with delicate china and filigreed silver, place cards using period images create a lovely, turn-of-the-century table.

Place Cards

Decorative Box

When used in decoupage, vintage images turn a simple box into a bright, pretty package. Add decorative trim and a tea-dyed tag for extra elegance.

Painting 101

Katie, Rusty and Oliver

original page

Each page in this book contains several possibilities to explore. The painting theme of this original page proves a perfect accompaniment to photos of a little artist and her companions.

Memories

2002

2. Bello, il più bello   Beautiful, the most beau-
                             tiful.

Many of the designs in this
book invite you to replace
portions of the original image
with personal photographs,
sentiments, and journaling.
The oval motif on this vintage
advertisement makes a perfect
frame for a cherished photo.

original page

Dress'en Up

An antique playbill is an unusual but sophisticated backdrop for a scrapbook page of young starlets. Muted, aged colors invite sepia-toned photographs.

original page

Lauren and Kayla

A Merry Christmas AND Happy New Year

From

Christmas

8

VALLEY FORGE

Christmas

USA 13c

Christmas 6 U.S.

Christmas 10c U.S.

Carrier and Ives

Christmas 6 U.S.

1975

KOCH & BRO.,

(Successors to L. D. Krause,)

805 Hamilton St., Allentown, Pa.

CHAMPION BOOT & SHOE STORE,

REPAIRING NEATLY DONE.

Ah! this is a lovely fit, whose make are they?

SULLERS & C.

and they will wear splendidly.

JOHN W. VREELAND,

Boots and Shoes,

Seneca Falls, N. Y.

SH01-004   SH01-003   SH01-002

SH01-005   SH01-015

SH01-006   SH01-016   SH01-014

SH01-007   SH01-013

                                              SH01-012

SH01-008   SH01-009   SH01-011

                                              SH01-010

CARTE POSTALE

Correspondance   Adresse

Motorcycle
1913
USA 5c

20 cents. Cotton for
, 55

U.S. POSTAGE

RE
als
for
wo
stamped on the same

NOLAN BROS.,
FINE SHOES,
Phelan Building,
SAN FRANCISCO.

LE CALCUL.

Copyright 1882 by Marques, Gair & Bailey.

oom in the Palace.
LLIUS, and Ladies
: he so troubles

acious

aliciously In
Believe this cra
So sovereignly b
I have lov'd thee
Leon. Make t
Dost think I am
To appoint m
purit

Not l
yet black brow
est; so that there
ut in a semicircle,
ith a pen.
Who taught yo
f women

SH02-003   SH02-002

                          SH02-008

SH02-004   SH02-007

                     SH02-009

SH02-005   SH02-006

SH03-003

SH03-004

SH03-002

SH03-010

SH03-011

SH03-012

SH03-005

SH03-009

SH03-013

SH03-006

SH03-008

03 — SH03-001

SH03-007

PHOTOGRAPHER'S DAILY COMPANION.

DISTANCES BEYOND WI RE IN FOCUS WHEN SHARP FO SECURED ON INFINITY.

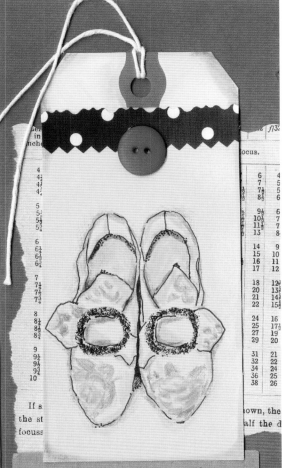

Your new shoes

CARD 25—Answer is top number over.

X
9
4

SH04-002

SH04-004   SH04-003

SH04-005

SH04-006

SH04-007   SH04-011

SH04-010

SH04-009

SH04-008

04 — SH04-001

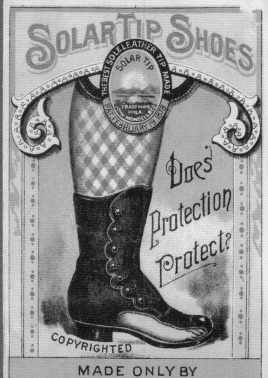

The Dish That Made France Famous

SHE is making the *pot-au-feu*, which might so easily be a commonplace soup if it were not a *chef d'œuvre*...

SH05-006

SH05-005

SH05-004

SH05-003   SH05-002

SH05-007

SH05-008   SH05-011

SH05-009

SH05-010

05 — SH05-001

Milano, 3 ottobre 1909.

Caro Giulio,

Stamani ho ricevuto il tuo bigliettino in cui mi
racconti ciò ch
avere maggior
a trovarti vers
che mi sia pos
Napoli ed ho
più presto. A
Saluti co

Gentilissima

Mi permetto con la presente pregarla di volere
cortesemente indicarmi quando posso venire a trovarla
per mostrarle il quadro di cui l e parlai altre volte. Se
Ella può ricevermi lunc   i essere da

Costura
de
1.5 cm.

Center front
Milieu du devant
Centro del frente

5 ft.

SH06-003   SH06-002

SH06-004

SH06-005

SH06-006   SH06-010

SH06-007

SH06-008

06 — SH06-001   SH06-009

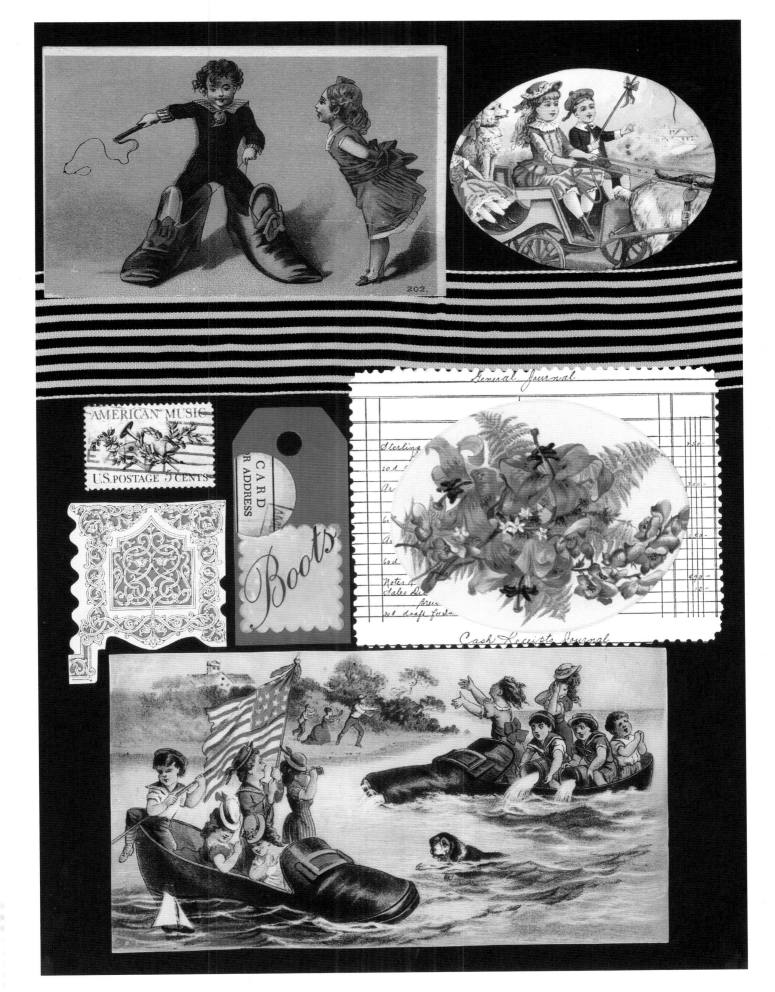

SH07-003

SH07-002

SH07-004

SH07-005

SH07-009

SH07-006

SH07-010

SH07-008

SH07-007

07 — SH07-001

soprabito, overcoat.
seduto, seduta, seated

65

the people.
ore.

SH08-003   SH08-002

SH08-004   SH08-010   SH08-009

SH08-005   SH08-011

SH08-006   SH08-007   SH08-008

08 — SH08-001

group of free citizens, oligarchy tended to prevail. The
eneral body of citizens had no control over the city gov-

BROWN'S FRENCH DRESSING AND SATIN POLISH.

For Ladies' and Children's Boots and Shoes.

rithout significant executive power. Municipal aut...

BUTTON'S RAVEN GLOSS SHOE DRESSING

KEEP YOUR 👁 OPEN.

Presented by
Melcher & Miller

A.S.T.Cº

Sign of
Gold Boot.

FOR EXPLANATION OF ⟨A.S.T.Cº⟩ SEE OTHER SIDE.

Button's RAVEN GLOSS SHOE DRESSING   TRADE MARK

SH09-003

SH09-002

SH09-008

SH09-007

SH09-006

SH09-004

SH09-005

G. W. GREENHILL
237 5th Ave.,
nearly opp. P. O. | 024 4th St.
CLINTON, IA.

REYNOLDS BROTHERS.
FINE SHOES, UTICA, N.Y.

$2 black robin

I LOVE SHOES

STANDARD TIP SHOES

Sold by HOBART, WOOD & CO.,
SAN FRANCISCO, CAL.

THE DAISY SHOE

THE BEST SOLE LEATHER TIP MADE

SOLAR TIP

TRADE MARK IN U.S.
PATENTED 1877

SOLAR TIP SHOES

MADE ONLY BY
JOHN MUNDELL
PHILAD. & Co.

SOLAR TIP BRIGADE

SH10-004   SH10-003   SH10-002

SH10-005

SH10-006 SH10-007

SH10-008

SH10-009   SH10-010

Sommer & Kaufmann

annual summe... SAL...

Next week ... ... added and further red... prevail, ar ... ...ee how ... ...can stay away from ... There ... ...mber of ... ... Ladies' Shoes. Total... former ... ... cost, we o... ...em at prices which, under ...

NOLAN BROS. FINE SHOES.
PHELAN'S BUILDING, S. F.

LOVE IS SLEEPING.

A alw... Lace ... s ... Lace ... Lace ... Lace ... La ...

Cloth tops, Ladies' *Kid Lace with Canary* Cloth tops.

be fitted up to 11 o'clock only and cannot be returned.

Ladies' ... ton — Canary Cloth tops.

Some Typical So...

Ladies' *Golden Nubu...* ly $12.00, now ...
Ladies' *Golden Nubu...* $12.00, now ...
Ladies' *Patent Colt* buck tops—
Ladies' *Brown Nubuck To...* now ...
Ladies' *Black... Kid tops*—
Ladies' *Blac... Lace* (as ... *Cloth tops*— now ...
L...

Fawn Buck tops—
Formerly $7.50 . . $5.65

JOHN KELLY'S FINE SHOES, ROCHESTER, N.Y.

...en Values in WHITE SHOES
...nvas Lace Shoes, turned soles,

near Stockton

near Geary

SH11-002

SH11-003   SH11-009

SH11-004   SH11-008

SH11-005   SH11-007

SH11-006

11 — SH11-001

VIEWS OF NEW YORK.
A few Broadway Earth-Scrapers.

In Style All The While

What do you think of these?

SH12-003

SH12-004

SH12-002

SH12-005

SH12-012

SH12-011

SH12-010

SH12-009

SH12-006

SH12-007

SH12-008

SH12-001

SH13-004   SH13-003   SH13-002

            SH13-005

                                    SH13-015   SH13-014

            SH13-006   SH13-013

SH13-007

SH13-008

                        SH13-011   SH13-012

SH13-009   SH13-010

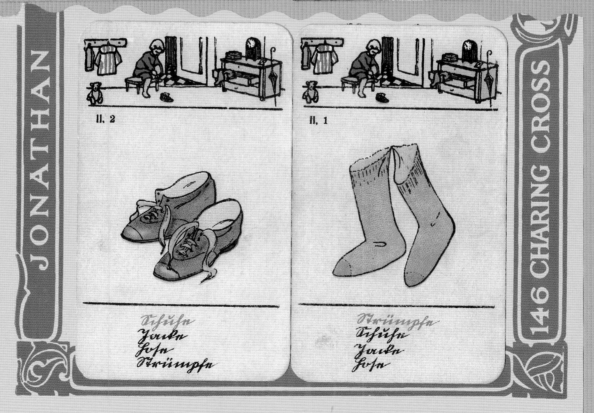

SH14-003   SH14-002

                                              SH14-010

SH14-004

SH14-005   SH14-009

SH14-006   SH14-007   SH14-008

14   SH14-001

EDWIN C. BURT,
FINE SHOES.

Presented by
A. J. CAMMEYER,
189 Sixth Avenue.
Cor. 12th St., one block from Macy's,
NEW YORK.

Copyright by A. B. Seeley 1881

NEW YORK CITY.
DEALER IN BOOTS AND SHOES
OF EVERY DESCRIPTION,

Shoes

ROMEO ET JULIETTE

Ens   ayons au bout du monde,
                       ans une paix profonde
                       os cœurs amoureux,
                  heur   Misses' and Children's Sandals
                   nté,   Chocolate Color
                                       Misses' and Children's
                  ar de   Strap Sandals, made
                                       from a choice selection
Rom. (chancelant) Ah,   of chocolate Vici kid,
                                       over the narrow
entrailles de pierr   coin last
                       are hand turned, making them very flexible and
                       easy. Widths, C, D, E and EE. Weight about 10 oz.
                       No. 46524 Sizes, 11½, 12, 12½, 13, 13½, 1, 1½ and 2.
                       Price, per pair...........................$1.00

THE ECONOMICAL COBBLER

59 CENTS FOR A $1.50 OUTFIT.

IT IS CHEAP, GOOD AND A GREAT TIME AND MONEY SAVER.

THE ECONOMICAL COBBLER

Contains all the Tools
Necessary for Shoe
Repairing . . . .

Contents:

COMPLETE
COBBLER'S
OUTFIT FOR
59 CENTS.

1 Iron Stand for Lasts
1 Last for Men's Work
1 Last for Boys' Work
1 Last for Children's Work
1 Shoemaker's Hammer
1 Shoemaker's Knife
1 Patent Peg Awl Handle
1 Peg Awl
1 Sewing Awl Handle
1 Sewing Awl
1 Harness Awl Handle
1 Harness Awl
1 Paper Heel Nails
1 Paper Half-soling Nails
1 Wrench for Peg Awl Handle
1 Copy Directions for Half-soling

ECONOMICAL
COBBLER

No. 47409 Securely packed in wooden box. Weight, 14 pounds.

Per single set $0.65
Six sets for 3.75
Twelve sets for 5.00

"Thank you," said I.
"What for?" with a raise of the eyebrows.
"For showing epigrams their proper place."

CENTRAL AVENUE
Boot and Shoe Manufactory.
478 CENTRAL AVENUE,
Near Congress St.   JERSEY CITY,
Gent's, Ladies' and Youth's Shoes
Constantly on hand. Repairing neatly
done. All orders promptly attended to
WALTERS, Supt.

STANDARD SCREW FASTENED
BOOTS AND SHOES
HAVE NO EQUAL

MY PAPA
IS GOING TO BUY ME A PAIR OF
STANDARD SCREW FASTENED SHOES
HE SAYS:
„They are Best in the World"

OVER

SH15-003

SH15-002

SH15-004

SH15-005

SH15-006   SH15-013

SH15-012

SH15-007

SH15-011

SH15-008

SH15-010

SH15-009

15 — SH15-001

Young,

RFIELD

g-gie

spright-ly than

Where we sat in the long, long a - go.
But — time a - lone was the pen.—

EMPRESS

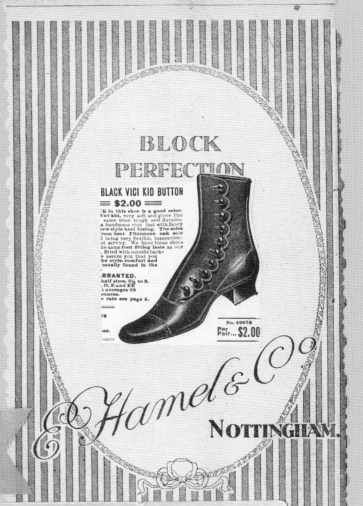

BLOCK PERFECTION

BLACK VICI KID BUTTON
$2.00

K in this shoe is a good selec-
Vici kid, very soft and glove like
same time tough and durable.
a handsome coin last with fancy
new style heel foxing. The soles
rom best Flintstone oak sole
d being very flexible, insure com-
d service. We have these shoes
he same foot fitting lasts as our
fitted with outside back-
e assure you that you
he style, comfort and
usually found in the

RRANTED.
half sizes, 2½ to 8.
, D, E and EE
t averages 29
ounces.
e rate see page 4.

No. 46076
Per....$2.00
Pair...

Hamel & Co
NOTTINGHAM.

SH16-002

SH16-010

SH16-003

SH16-009

SH16-008

SH16-004

SH16-007

SH16-011   SH16-006

SH16-005

SH16-001

5
9

Dem. Not so, my lord; for his valour cannot carry his discretion; and the fox carries the goose.
The. His discretion, I am sure, cannot carry his valour; for the goose carries not the fox. It is well: leave it to his discretion, and let us listen to the moon.
Moon. This lantern doth the horned moon present:
             [head.
Dem. He should have worn the horns on his
The. He is no crescent, and his horns are invisible within the circumference.
Moon. This lantern doth the horned moon present;
         present;
Myself the man i' the

CARTE POSTALE

*214
A woman who has on a new pair of low shoes never gets the edge of her skirt soiled.*

Shiny new shoes

SH17-004

SH17-003

SH17-002

SH17-005

SH17-011

SH17-012

SH17-010

SH17-006

SH17-009

SH17-013

SH17-007

SH17-008

17 — SH17-001

SH18-003   SH18-002

SH18-004   SH18-007

SH18-005   SH18-006

SH18-001

Dreaming

song

BY

...CISE...

BY

...LLEY...

Ç. ANTON

SH19-002

SH19-003   SH19-008

SH19-004   SH19-005   SH19-006   SH19-007

19 — SH19-001

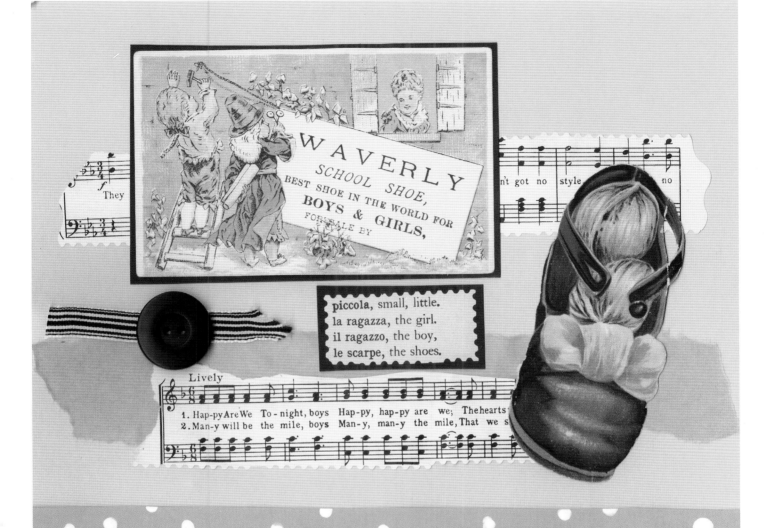

WAVERLY
SCHOOL SHOE,
BEST SHOE IN THE WORLD FOR
BOYS & GIRLS,
FOR SALE BY

They

n't got no style   no

piccola, small, little.
la ragazza, the girl.
il ragazzo, the boy,
le scarpe, the shoes.

Lively

1. Hap-py Are We To-night, boys Hap-py, hap-py are we; The hearts
2. Man-y will be the mile, boys Man-y, man-y the mile, That we s

THERE WAS AN OLD WOMAN WHO LIVED

1234   30536
WAS A.   OE89
6789.   42678
IVED   SHOE
7418   45678
            MAN WI.

'THERE WAS AN
OLD WOMAN WHO
LIVED IN A SHOE.'

—Sois sage.

SH20-003

SH20-002

SH20-004   SH20-012   SH20-011   SH20-010

SH20-009

SH20-013

SH20-005

SH20-006   SH20-008

SH20-007

20 — SH20-001

WRIGHT.   A. W. DONOVAN.

The girl has SHOES

E·T·WRIGHT & Co.

MANUFACTURERS OF

The Just Wright SHOE

Rockland, Mass.   12/19,

SINGLE PAIRS, 50 CENTS EXTRA
SINGLE PAIRS, TO MEASURE, $1 EXTRA.

LESROOM,
STREET.

JOSEPH KOHLBECHER
Our Own Manufacture

Terms;
2/30   net 60
Do not pay our agents on our account.

Sold to   C. Sautter

Remit direct to Rockland, Mass., in Boston or New York Funds.

Case No.		Pairs.	
1	1504	24	un et b
2	1508		
3	1512		El
3	1640		Belt
2	1649		But
3	1649	1	
3	1656	10	
3	1661	10	
1	1662	12	

SOLAR TIP SHOES
MADE ONLY BY JOHN MUNDELL & CO. PHILAD.A
NONE GENUINE WITHOUT THE TRADEMARK
SOLE LEATHER TIP MADE
SOLAR TIP
THE PAT.D FEBRUARY 19, 1878.
SOLAR TIP
I WISH I HAD SOLAR TIPS
SOLD BY

THE
...ping Shoe House,
PHELAN BUILDING,
SAN FRANCISCO.

RAVEN GLOSS
BUTTON'S RAVEN GLOSS
FOR DRESSING LADIES AND CHILDREN'S SHOES
VALISES, HARNESS &c.
Eugene L. Button
MANUFACTURED BY BUTTON & OTTLEY NEW YORK

SH21-003   SH21-002

                        SH21-009

SH21-004   SH21-008

SH21-005

SH21-006   SH21-007

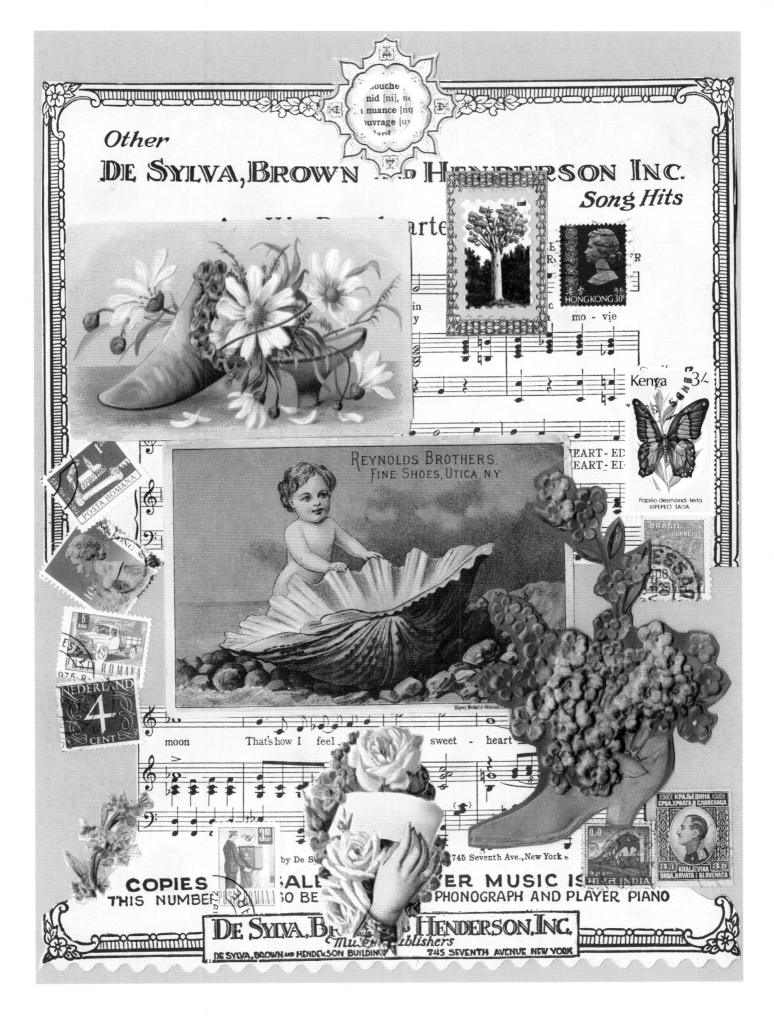

SH22-003   SH22-002

SH22-004   SH22-019

SH22-018

SH22-005

SH22-017

SH22-006   SH22-020   SH22-016

SH22-015

SH22-007

SH22-014

SH22-008   SH22-011   SH22-013

SH22-009   SH22-012

SH22-010

22 SH22-001

FOUNDED 1854

THE
British Journal of Photography

SH23-002

SH23-003

SH23-004

SH24-002

SH24-003

SH24-004

SH24-005

SH24-006

24 ── SH24-001

SH25-002

SH25-003   SH25-008

                        SH25-009   SH25-007

SH25-004   SH25-005   SH25-006

JOHN W. VREELAND,
Boots and Shoes,
Seneca Falls, N. Y.

fight this roy
ou hast unw

an to wish
God be with

MONTJOY
me to kr

lt now
overthro
near the
glutted

thou w
e; that
a swee
ere, wr

s safe home,
is nam'd,
pian.
old age

K. Hen. Who hath se
Mont. The constable of France
K. Hen. I pray thee, bear my f

then s
y mock

the lio
kill'd w

no dou
e whic'
this
valia

ried in

here the

ing up t
choke y
reed a

r in our
bullet's
se of mi
y.
the const
working-
all besm
ainful fie
in our ho
ill not fly
lovenry:
re in the
yet ere nip
they will
French s

f they do t
my ransom
save thou

JOHN W. VREELAND,
Boots and Shoes,
Seneca Falls, N. Y.

SH26-003

SH26-002

SH26-004

SH26-007

SH26-005

SH26-006

26

SH26-001

Carte Postale

Correspondance

Adresse

792.

14

Bluebird
PEARL BUTTONS
© IOWA P. B CO. 1923

The green grove
They say we a
D.S. And now we a

bird's wings,
sapphire ly-

ruiseñor

the _ dai-sies _ sprung;
by the white breakers flung,
als of life near-ly done,

SH27-003   SH27-002

SH27-004

SH27-005

SH27-011   SH27-010

SH27-009

SH27-006   SH27-007

SH27-008

Presented by
PREBLE BROS.,
DEALERS IN
FINE BOOTS AND SHOES,

To my Love with my love

J. N. GLOYES
FINE SHOES.
Utica, N.Y.

Wedding

Wishes

Only my wish on a simple card.
But if wishes all come true:
There's health and wealth and truest of friends.
And the best of luck for you.

Please ac____ subje___, the ___ qua___ s sta___ they a. All B___ ___ject
for 12 to ___ subje___, the ___ qua___ s sta___ they a. All B___ S 1

BRIDE POSTCARDS 9 PRO
:: OR

OCHROME.   CREAM TONED.   LEIGHTON GLOSSY.   RUBENS MATT.   KEY
EE COLOUR.   POYNTER CARBON.   COLLOTYPE.   PHOTOGRA
ICES PER 1000. BLOCKS EXTRA for first edition only of any subject. FULL CARD BLOC
mprint of 24 letters included; MARGINAL BLOCKS 13 1 each, 12 words of type title allowed.
VORDS *in type*, ½d. each.   De Luxe Blocks 20

2 MONOCHROME	3 LEIGHTON ___TER		5 THREE COLOUR				6 CREAM TONE
Sepia, black or Green.	GLOSS or RUBE MAT		from Coloured Objects. Paintings, Designs, &c. or KEYTINT				POSTCARD
NORMAL DISPATCH			ORDINARY GLOSSY P.O.P. or Bromides.				↑
Per 1000 cards, "full cards" or marginal.	Per 1000 car___		a b c d				MOST ARTISTIC RESULTS
Blocks extra. as column 1.	Blocks extr___ as colum___		___cks 1000 5000 10000				
£ s. d.	£ s. d.		s. d.	s. d.	s. d.	s. d.	7/-
1 4 0	1 16 0					41 0	per 1000 ext___
1 5 6	1 17 6			48 6	43 6		to prices in
1 6 2	1 18 2	2 ___ 6		55 0	48 0	45 0	cols. 2, 3 &
1 6 8	2 1 6	2 6 6	3 17 3	60 0	52 0		
1 7 0	2 2 0	2 10 6				50 6	
1 7 8	2 7 8	2 16 6	8 8 0				

1 - 11 - 8
One-day BLOCKS :
"Full card" 17 4
Marginal 14 5

Printing name or SPECIAL MATTER on address side, 8/6 down to 2/6 per 1000
amount of matter and quantity ordered.

All Blocks become Customers' property, and are sent along with th___
we are asked to store them.   ☞ **PRICES** for other quantities on ___

MALL QUANTITIES.—(Blocks extra. as
___-any monochrome colour: 100 10/-1
19/10.

DISPATCH " means 21 DAYS

Postcards in LARGE QUANTITIES.—(Se___
blocks or electros must be ordered for the larg___
Per subject. Full Card, not boxed —2,000 to 4,00___
to 9,000, 25/8; 10,000, 25/-: 20,000, 24/4; 50,000,
23/-; 300,000, 22/8; 1,000,000, 22/2

SH28-003

SH28-002

SH28-004

SH28-005

SH28-006

SH28-008

SH28-007

28 SH28-001

SH29-004   SH29-002

                                        SH29-003

SH29-005

SH29-006

SH29-007   SH29-013   SH29-012

SH29-008   SH29-014

SH29-009

SH29-010   SH29-011

29 — SH29-001

The Comfort of Well-Dressed Feet

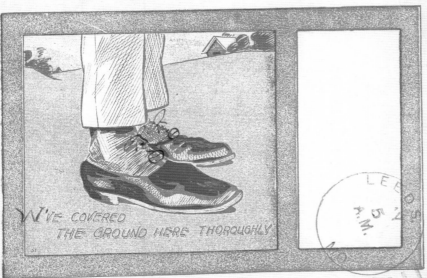

WE'VE COVERED THE GROUND HERE THOROUGHLY

SH30-003   SH30-002

                                    SH30-007

SH30-004   SH30-005   SH30-006

Lewis P. Ross

Manufacturer & Wholesale Dealer in

Boots, Shoes, Rubbers & Findings.

Rochester, N.Y. Dec. 5, 1898.

60-62-64-
G. G.
Dictated

Take my best wishes!
May each birthday
bring
Joy in its sunshine
health upon its wing

$18.

short of paying the bills

, which occurred   your   ke only Gree

for instance if aliti had   ery elegant
friend
might b goo   rned
lorious b   nce

regular   ed,

disco   d at 5%, or 94   c

atl   lige.

WES   REEN,
e Sho
Cor   and Charapa Sts.

John Cavanagh & Son,
HEADQUARTERS FOR
BOOTS AND SHOES
BOONVILLE, N.Y.

hrons, Lace, Boston,

the buckle only.

DEC 21 1898

SH31-002

SH31-003

SH31-004   SH31-008

SH31-005

SH31-009

SH31-006

SH31-007

CARTE POSTALE

SCHOOL SHOES

MANUFACTURED BY
Phelps, Dodge & Palmer Co. of Chicago.

SOULIERS

SH32-003   SH32-002

                                                              SH32-007

          SH32-004   SH32-008

        SH32-005
                                    SH32-006

32 — SH32-001

Bonne année

Illingworth's
PHOTOGRAPHIC
PAPERS
& POST CARDS

¹shoe \'shü\ *n* **1** : a covering for the human foot **2** : HORSESHOE **3** : the part of a brake that presses on the wheel **4** : the casing of an automobile tire
²shoe *vb* **shod** \'shäd\ *also* **shoed** \'shüd\; **shoe·ing** \'shü-iŋ\ : to put a shoe or shoes on
shoe·lace \-ˌlās\ *n* : a lace or string for fastening a shoe
shoe·mak·er \-ˌmā-kər\ *n* : one who makes or repairs shoes
shoe·string \'shü-ˌstriŋ\ *n* **1** : SHOELACE **2** : a small sum of money

SH33-003

SH33-002

SH33-004   SH33-009

SH33-005

SH33-006

SH33-007   SH33-008

33 — SH33-001

iew Drill 2

...structions for
...le space.

...b. Ne...
...3 mixe...
No. 1 d...
...rn Manit...
...3 Northe...

TESTS

Top ma... ...d 70; t...
copy. Si... ...each qu...
Double s... ...ent the...
of each... ...iage pr...
Review i...

...ryone excels in something in which another
...Publius Syrus

...one is born into t... ...ose work is not
...ith him.--James Russ...

...e one thing that m... ...artist is a
clear perception and a fi... ...in distinc-
tion from that imperfect m... ...and uncertain
...the f... ...res and the lumpy
...artisa... ...s or in stone.--

...k errors, record results, improve skill

Su...

...inches
...few tri...
page 35, for explanat...
margin. Double space

...sked t...
...n all
...ing.
...d none
...is war...
...er-cov...

French Embossed.

H. N. AYRES.
→❋ BOOTS AND SHOES ❋←
7 STERLING BLOCK,
BRIDGEPORT, CONN.

Compliments of
FERGUSON & REEVE,
DEALERS IN GROCERIES, BOOTS & SHOES,
ASHTON, DAKOTA.

SH34-002

SH34-004   SH34-003

SH34-010   SH34-009

SH34-005   SH34-011

SH34-008

SH34-006   SH34-007

SH34-001

SH35-003   SH35-002

SH35-004   SH35-010

SH35-005

                                                      SH35-009

                                                                SH35-008

SH35-006   SH35-007

35 SH35-001

GLOVES & MITTEN

MANUFAC

MILWAUKEE, WIS.

10/11/21 315

CO.'S

2378 A LEGEN

Y.10

QUARTETS SUITABLE FOR CHORUS

2351 Now, O now, I needs must part   J. Dowland   10
15
10
es 12
12
12
10

15
15
10
15
12
12
15
10
12
15
10

N. MacDougall
Manufacturer of and Dealer in
BOOTS & SHOES,
No. 3008 Mission St.

1. Tu finis.
2. Vo
3. Ils
4. Fûtes-vous?
5. Ils   aient
6. Qu'   ons.
7. Je meus.
8. Je
9. I
10. Qu'   yassen

2391 The Three Friends   R. L. de Pearsall   10
2392 A Slumber Song   F. N. Löhr   12
2393 O night most beautiful   J. L. Roeckel   12
        of Richmond Hill   J. Hook-Leslie   12
        sun is sinking   J. Hook-Leslie   10
        the Garden   J. Hook-Leslie   12
        f but within thee   G. Durant   10
                                              B. Luard Selby   10
                                              F. N. Löhr   12
        e of Love   H. Hofmann   25

(Prices apply to U. S. A.)

mer, Inc., New York

Copyrighted by M.P.Tobin, N.Y. 1883

SH36-003   SH36-002

SH36-004   SH36-009

                                 SH36-010 SH36-008

                                          SH36-007

SH36-005   SH36-006

SH37-004

SH37-003

SH37-002

SH37-005

SH37-006

SH37-007

SH37-012

SH37-008

SH37-011

SH37-009

SH37-010

SH37-001

pose to relieve and follow them,—
fled, not having struck one
ew the general wreck an
were they with their
alloon, to win the
albot with a spe
France, with
ength,
presume to
Talbot sl
idly her
ch a wo
dastard
O no
d Scale
rd:
he res
lis ra
y:
the
rone,—
shall
heir lord
my ma
n Franc
our great
sand soldi
loody, d
ake
So
g'd
ish gro
of
lly
w so
in
rdain'd his special governor;
his safety there I'll best devise. [Exit.

Birthday Regards

yoke.
re take my
[Exit.
the haste I
ry king.
[Exit.
where the young

So in the earth, to this day is not
did he shine upon the Englis
victors, upon us he sr
any moment but
ve lie near Orlea
mish'd Englis

our in a r
r porrid

like n
d to t
dro
why

t
'd
en
o n
w

for
kill
he fo

wards
çon, R

aw the lik
stards! I wou
eft me midst my
ury is a desperate
as one weary of his l
The other lords, like lions wanti
Do rush upon us as their hungry
    Alen. Froissart, a countryma
        cords,
England all Olivers and Rowlan
During the time Edward the T
More truly now may this be ve
For none but Samsons and Goli
It sendeth forth to skirmish. On
Lean raw-bon'd rascals! who woul
        pose
They had such courage and audacity
    Char. Let's leave this town; for th
        hair-brain'd slaves,
And hunger will enforce them to be more eage

'Tis luck to find a horse's shoe,
And here is wishing luck to you!

Bonne Année

SH38-003   SH38-002

                    SH38-009   SH38-008   SH38-007

SH38-004

SH38-005   SH38-006

SH38-001

SH39-003

SH39-004

SH39-005   SH39-002

                                                 SH39-009

              SH39-010

SH39-006   SH39-011   SH39-008

              SH39-007

SH39-001

Presents

SPRINGTIME IN MAYO

Nous épirons votre réveil, enfin de ce lourd sommeil. Je te la... ...ui, Courage...et sa
Et vous fuirez aux bras de celui qui vous... ...égés, votre époux et moi... Ta d...

Melody-Drama

JUL. (taking...
, à votre main   And that...
LAW.
, demain.   JUL.   Till the hour...

TRIEME ACTE.   END OF THE...

ORDER BY
NUMBER

No. 46014, Black $2.50

Straight grain o
Droit-fil du tis
Hilo de la...

Sincerely
ck Wan

Línea del corte
Ligne de coupe
...e Cutting line
...e de couture

NO. 668
Sierra BUTTONS
WASHABLE
ROMEO ET JULIETTE—

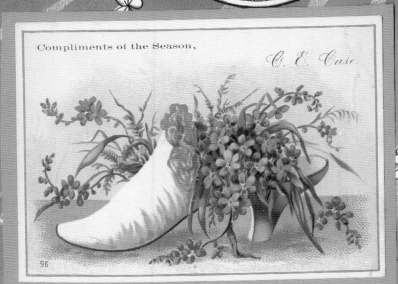

Compliments of the Season,

C. E. Case.

96

Springtime In Mayo....	.60
The Top Of The Morning...............	.60
A Bit O' The Brogue...	.60
Don't You Love To Dream Of Dear Old Ireland?.......	.60

SH40-002

SH40-003

SH40-004

SH40-005

SH40-006

SH40-008

SH40-007

SH40-001

SH41-002

SH41-003

SH41-004

SH41-005

41 — SH41-001

classico amatissimo —

Chaussure

No. 26

for piercing eyelet holes in t
want, so that I have less than
economical, and hoards her m
hundred francs! And I have on
punished. I could throw my
ful to me to wear it now. Po
Agathe was so nice about it. S
dred and fifty francs in our tw
you everything just as it happ
"D   gh   we mar
We   hoard
on   but
th   We
w   ha
sa   thi
si   hey
de   ra
A   litt
of   our
O   m
th   wi
w   r le
to   sid
a   th
                      in th
of   ge s
su   ch

No. 15

but strangers will enjoy a fai
tive lack pocket handkerchi
dowager Lady
and boxes '
ing bro
not, t
posa
des'

me where de   or-ange blos-soms

Paris

"Mademoiselle,"

amico, friend (m.)
amici, friends (m.)
amica, friend (f.)
amiche, friends (f.
la camera, the room.
il cappello, the hat.

Notch For view A, B or C ▼
Entaille Pour la vue A, B ou C
Piquete Para la vista A, B o C

SH42-003

SH42-004

SH42-002

SH42-005

SH42-011

SH42-006

SH42-010

SH42-007

SH42-008

SH42-009

42 — SH42-001

LOVE'S LABOUR'S LOST

Go to; thou hast it *ad dunghill*, at the fingers' | *Moth.* An excellent

─GO TO─

H. CLARK'S THE RELIABLE Shoe Dealer

FOR YOUR BOOTS AND SHOES,

79 East Main S⟨...⟩ ⟨Am⟩sterdam, N. Y.

SH43-005   SH43-004   SH43-003

SH43-002

SH43-006   SH43-012

SH43-013

SH43-014   SH43-011

SH43-007

SH43-010

SH43-015

SH43-009

43   SH43-001

SH43-008

Happy Are We

PRESENTED BY Gowdy & Remington,
SPRINGFIELD, MASS.

EDWIN C. BURT,
FINE SHOES.

SH44-002

SH44-004   SH44-003

SH44-005

SH44-006

SH44-009

SH44-007   SH44-010

SH44-008

44 — SH44-001

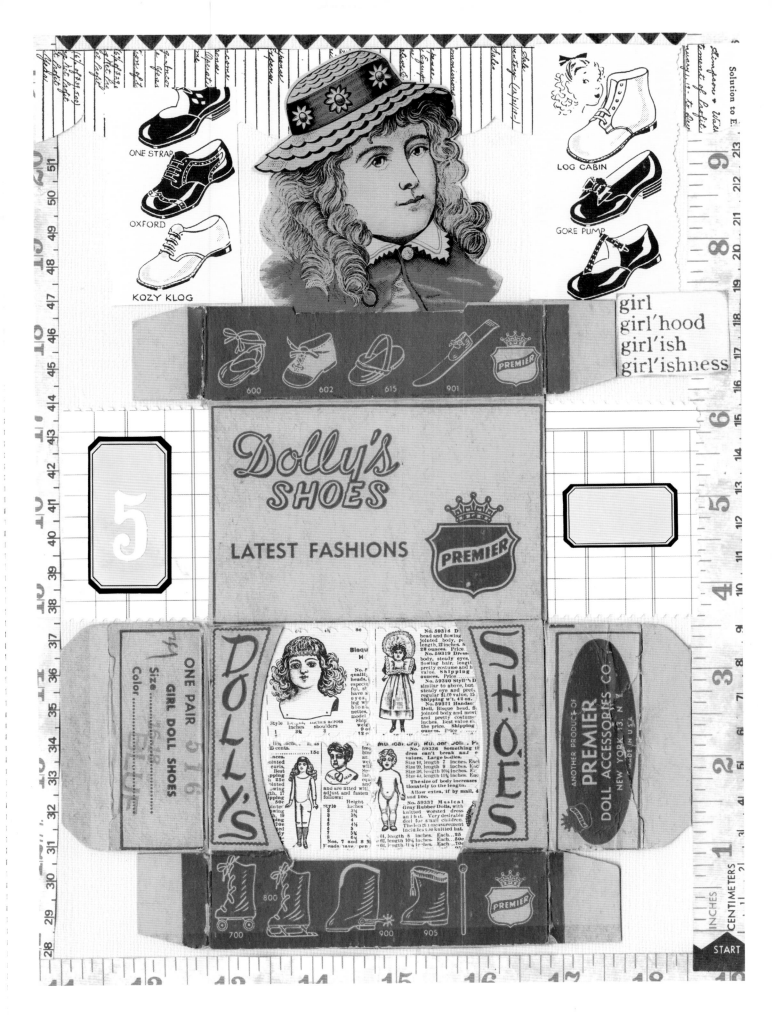

SH45-003

SH45-002

SH45-004

SH45-005

SH45-013

SH45-012

SH45-006

SH45-007

SH45-014

SH45-008

SH45-011

SH45-010

SH45-015   SH45-018

SH45-016   SH45-017

45   SH45-001

SH45-009

SH46-004　　　　　SH46-003

　　　　　　　　　　　　　　SH46-002

　　　　　　　　SH46-014

SH46-005　　　　　　　　　　　SH46-013

　　　　　　　　SH46-015

　　　　　　　　　　　　　SH46-012

SH46-006　　　　SH46-016

　　　　　　　　SH46-017　　　SH46-011

　　　SH46-007

SH46-008　　SH46-009　　SH46-010

A happy Birthday

COMPLIMENTS
JAMES M. MEADE,
FINE SHOES,
139 MYRTLE AVENUE,
BROOKLYN.

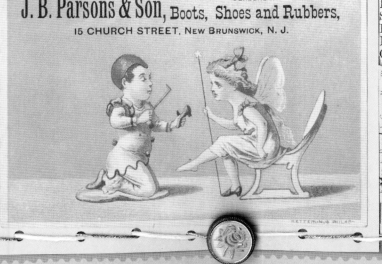

Ni larmes, ni prière.
..n, rien ne peut les attendrir...
...te des cieux, Juliette...—Et

...arir,—Ah, la fièvre t'égare
...toi quel délire s'empare?
...n aimé, Rappelle ta raison.

J. B. Parsons & Son, **DEALERS IN** Boots, Shoes and Rubbers,
15 CHURCH STREET, New Brunswick, N. J.

Console-toi, pauvre
Le rêve état trop beau
L'amour, céleste flamme,
Survit, même au tombeau
Il soulève la pierre,
Et des anges béni,
Comme un flot de lumière
Se perd dans l'infini...

19 rue de Verd...
Rosny... Boi...

SH47-002

SH47-004

SH47-005   SH47-003

SH47-006

SH47-007

SH47-008

SH47-009   SH47-011

SH47-010

SH47-001

SH48-002

SH48-004   SH48-003

SH48-005

SH48-012

SH48-011

SH48-006   SH48-013

SH48-010

SH48-007   SH48-008   SH48-009

48 ─| SH48-001 |

BUY C.M. HENDERSON & C°S
CELEBRATED BOOTS & SHOES

CHICAGO

souliers

LIMITED,
ssors to   Largest Co   ers in

B   ES,
WOTTON-UN   GLOS., ENG.

Paris, 6 mai 1934

CARTE POSTALE

CERTAINS PAYS ÉTRANGERS N'ACCEPTENT PAS LA CORRESPONDANCE DE CE COTÉ (se renseigner à la poste)

Chère Belle-Maman,

CORRESPONDANCE   **ADRESSE**

*Nous avons été contents de recevoir de
notre lettre ce matin au réveil, merci. -
Hélène (dite Cacchy-Caurreau) vous
répondra demain, mais en attendant
je viens vous annoncer si vous ne
voulez pas vous ... que
Lucie, à ... Lucie
Derkiste ... ...
aura ... ... de vacances
dont ... ...*

SH49-003

SH49-004   SH49-002

                                                  SH49-009

                          SH49-010   SH49-008

                                    SH49-007

SH49-005

                          SH49-006

— SH49-001

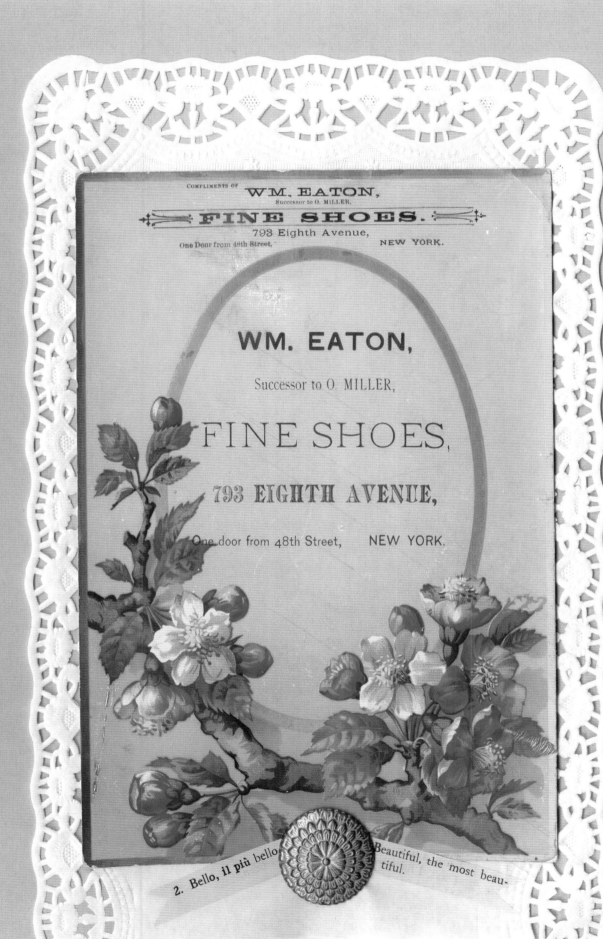

COMPLIMENTS OF WM. EATON,
Successor to O. MILLER,

FINE SHOES.

793 Eighth Avenue,
One Door from 48th Street, NEW YORK.

WM. EATON,

Successor to O. MILLER,

FINE SHOES,

793 EIGHTH AVENUE,

One door from 48th Street, NEW YORK.

2. Bello, il più bello. Beautiful, the most beautiful.

SH50-002

SH50-003

SH50-004

SH50-005

SH50-006

SH50-001

A happy
Birthday

Tom Soto

A Kindly Greeting.

CARTE POSTALE

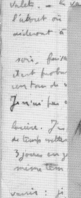

SH51-004   SH51-003

                                                                    SH51-002

        SH51-005

                        SH51-009

SH51-006

    SH51-007

                        SH51-008

Compliments of

J. D. McDONALD,
Boots and Shoes,
58 State Street   Rochester, N. Y.
Agent for Burt's Fine Shoes, and Grover's Soft Shoes.

Bonne Année

SH52-003

SH52-002

SH52-004

SH52-008

SH52-005

SH52-006

SH52-007

SH52-001

Romeo et Juliette

Presented by ANDREW ALEXANDER,
6th Ave. and 23d St., New York.

EDWIN C. BURT   FINE SHOES   over

FRENCH=ENGLISH EDITION.

20 S. Eighth Street,
PHILADELPHIA.

EDWIN C. BURT, Fine Shoes   over

SH53-002

SH53-003

SH53-004

SH53-005   SH53-008

SH53-009

SH53-007

SH53-006

SH53-001

for the
Par........le

R

Jeweler........ilversmith

384 Fourteenth Street
Near Franklin

TRULY
THINE.

SH54-003

SH54-002

SH54-004

SH54-007

SH54-005

SH54-006

SH54-001

ALL FOR THEE.

Thou knowest
That for thee, only,
My heart burns
With love's flame.
All silently
I tremble,
At the mention
Of thy name!
Oh, turn not
From such loving;
Believe, that
Heart of thine,
Will never
Find another,
To love with
Love like mine!

550		[1920
DIVIDE T...		FOCUS OF
If the quotient...		The angle is
		Degrees.
0·282		66
0·3		67
0·317		68
0·335		69
0·353		70
0·37		71
0·389		72
0·407		73
0·425		74
0·443		75
0·462		76
0·48		77
0·5		78
0·517		79
0·536		80
0·555		81
0·573		82
0·592		83
0·611		84
0·631		85
0·65		86
0·67		87
0·689		88
0·708		89
0·728		90

Example.—Given a lens of 13 inches equivalent focus; required the angle included by it on plate $3\frac{1}{4} \times 4\frac{1}{4}$.

Diagonal is 5·3 inches. $5·3 \div 13 = ·407$, corresponding with angle of 23°.

Fancy Shoes

COMPLIMENTS OF ——
K. HUNSTABLE,
—Manufacturer and Dealer in—
✦ BOOTS AND SHOES, ✦
732 Elm St., DALLAS, TEXAS.

C-675

John S. Griffith.

shoes

SH55-004

SH55-002

SH55-003

SH55-013 SH55-012

SH55-011

SH55-005

SH55-010

SH55-009

SH55-006 SH55-007 SH55-008

55 SH55-001

The   old rust-y mill is
But to me you're as fair as you
of the days that are g

ve - ning, When the bells are

ing! Ding, dong, ding, dong, ding, dong.

SH56-003   SH56-002

                                          SH56-010

        SH56-004   SH56-009

SH56-005   SH56-006   SH56-007

                                   SH56-008

SH56-001

SH57-002

SH57-003   SH57-006

SH57-004

SH57-005

57   SH57-001